Earth To Heaven & Back

By
Violet Tasker

Transition or Death

Something we all must
go through
alone

or so we are told

This book will place
healthy doubts in your
mind.

© COPYRIGHT V.W. TASKER 1998

All rights reserved. No part of this book may be reproduced, stored in a retrieval system, or transmitted in any form by any means, whether electronic, mechanical, photocopying, recording, or otherwise, without prior written permission of Violet Tasker.

Formerly published under the title "Transition: A Peep Through The Veil" 1991 and 1993.

Reprint : 2005

ISBN 0-473-05589-9

The Copy Press, Nelson, New Zealand

This book is dedicated to
my daughter
KATHY
whose love, laughter and
teenage moods I will always
treasure

Thanks to my early teachers
Vicky, Nolene, Kay
For placing my feet on the
right path

And the many friends who have
encouraged me over
the years.

ABOUT THE AUTHOR

Violet was born in England during the second World War and was adopted out from one of the Welfare Homes at the age of seven. She travelled as a young mother to Africa and Australia, returning to England in the early seventies.

She, with her family, finally settled in New Zealand in 1977, where the sheer weight of evidence given her from beyond the veil prompted her to write the experiences down, in the hope that some people may find comfort in the knowledge that DEATH HAS NO STING.

THE AUTHOR'S NOTE

The age old questions still continue to bother the human consciousness, is there or is there not LIFE BEYOND DEATH? Can we, while still in the physical body, visit that place, where we are told no travellers return?

I was convinced that we could not until a few years ago when I was subjected to a remarkable introduction to the place I felt was out of bounds.

When this started I was 42 years old and even writing about it now, reliving the experiences, makes me wonder if, by recording them, my reader may feel some concern as to what may be reviewed within the pages.

Let me allay any fears now, this book is written solely to give a greater understanding of LIFE and DEATH.

We have life, therefore at some stage we must die. The comfort I have received from this other land of light over the years has prompted me to write and share all the knowledge I have gained.

The onset of the book deals with my early life and the first 15 years of marriage, please stay with it as these years are important to the experiences that follow later in the book.

The out of body visits to the spirit world only started in 1982, so the early years were starved of any knowledge.

Part One

Contents

PART ONE
1. The Early Years.

This tells of my life before the adoption, my information has been gathered from people who knew me at that time. I have deliberately left names out as I do not wish to cause any undue hurt to any remaining family or unknown relations who may still be alive.

2. The Family.

Here I introduce the family that I had been adopted into, there were three girls and one boy. The eldest of the girls was Roberta (Dolly), then came our only brother Michael (Micky), Camilla (known as Meal) and the youngest of the girls was Ernestina (Tina) four years my junior.

3. School Days and Marriage.

Jan was my special friend at school, later after her death she would teach me about the spirit world.
Here I meet my husband and with our son Stephen we move to Africa.

4. Africa.

The first suspicion of a spirit world is introduced to me, but unfortunately I ignored the signal.
The Bantu African were the people that had me questioning Spirit Healing.

5.   Australia.

Henty and our family became great friends until his death a few years ago.

6.   England.

I meet up with my old school friend Jan only to lose her, but my lessons in these other spirit worlds accelerate.

Easter Sunday 1990 and as I sit in the living room of the small but comfortable home my husband and I rent in Auckland, NewZealand, I reflect on the news I have just been given by my younger sister Tina.

She has told us that she has secondary cancer, she has already been through the battle of surgery and chemotherapy treatment and all that goes with it.

Now must be the time for me to put to print all I have gained in help and knowledge from the heavens or spirit world, that place we all go to at the end of our journey here on earth.

So many wait till death knocks at their door or the door of someone they love before they begin to question the reality of an afterlife.

Which is fair enough but we can gain some knowledge now while we are still in good health and have a sound mind.

When we go on a holiday, especially if the travelling will take us to a different land and culture than the one we are used to, we look to see if we have the right maps, clothing, whether we will be able to stomach the food and so on. Yet for our final journey we couldn't care less about such trivia.

That is why we become so frightened; nobody is quite sure what to expect. I'm not sure, but I have had a little introduction to that other world and I hope it will give you all something to think about.

Over the years I have become convinced that there must be more to life than the day to day struggle to earn the necessary coins to feed clothe and run a family unit.

We must all learn our own lessons, every experience that we have in life has a lesson there somewhere if only we could see it.

Oldchurch Hospital, Romford, Essex, England winter 1941, the maternity wards are far too busy with the many war babies being born, most of them from unmarried mothers.

These young girls having no idea whether they will ever see the fathers of their children again, I was one of the babies born during the winter of that year, the fathers, should they return from the horrors of war, would probably never visit the child let alone the mother.

Some, I guess, would not even realise that they had fathered a child. The majority of the babies were left at the hospitals, as I was, to be farmed out to the Welfare Homes. During the second World War there seemed to be a host of these Children's Homes springing up all over Britain.

The reason being to house these unwanted children resulting from the union of young girls and the passing servicemen.

My first recollection of being alive was at the Children's Court in Romford, on the day of my adoption, the month was May 1948. I remember being given some paper to draw on by a policewoman, while my new Mum and Dad were inside the Court Chambers with the Magistrate.

While I was busy with my drawing, which, I might add, I still have today, I heard a young woman crying hysterically. She was talking about her baby being taken from her. I was a child of seven at the time and I couldn't work out who had taken her baby. It made me very unhappy and I became as upset as she was, though I didn't cry.

Looking back, it may have been that the woman was not a fit mother or maybe it was a custody case, it could even have been the fact that a young girl was giving up her baby for adoption but didn't really want to part with it.

My adoption was allowed as my birth mother and my adopted mother were sisters. This I did not discover until I was in my early teens.

My birth mother had found a man she wanted to marry; they had decided not to take me out of the Welfare Home as they did not want children.

According to Mum, the last place I was fostered out to must have been awful. The main Welfare Home I had been placed in was Catholic, as I was of Catholic descent. Therefore I can only guess that the foster parents must have been Catholic.

When I arrived I was covered with sores and my hair was riddled with fleas, I also had strap marks on my body. I was hospitalised for a while to make me strong again.

Mum tells me I was petrified of cats and would scream and hide whenever I saw one. My toilet training was sadly neglected and I would hide in corners and do my business there. I guess I was a problem to them. I was seven at the time.

My father was a very handsome man, kind in many ways, but when he was in a foul mood, then watch out! Father was violent and very cruel. He would have us all at his beck and call, and heaven help anyone who dared question him. He had a cane and would use it on us when ever he thought we were out of line, according to his rules.

My mother was a gentle soul, dominated by her husband, but would forgive easily. She loved to dance and she would perform these marvellous acrobatics ending up in the splits, much the same as the gymnasts today. We all thought she was wonderful and loved to see her dance.

Mum married young and had her first child at sixteen, so any ambitions of becoming an international dancer with fame and fortune were soon shattered.

There were four children in the family already by the time I came to town, three girls and one boy.

The eldest was Roberta called Dolly, she always seemed to be the mother figure for us. Mum was always working long hours, among the jobs I can recall were: working in the Cinema as an usherette, on the buses as a Conductor and even as a Bar Maid. Consequently as she was working odd hours she would be tired in the mornings.

Doll would make sure we were clean, tidy and ready for school. She would cook our breakfast, which was always porridge, and make sure we had our dinner money in our hands before we all marched off to school.

My brother Michael, Micky, was the next on the family tree, he was always playing truant from school and Mum and Dad were forever searching the streets for him and dragging him back to school. In the end he was sent to a boarding school in Surrey.

Dad and us four girls would visit him once in a while on Dad's old motorbike which had a sidecar attached. Dolly would sit on the back of the bike and the rest of us girls would all cram into the sidecar. If you happened to be the unfortunate one to be chosen to sit right at the back of the sidecar, you would end up with your two sisters sitting on your outstretched legs for the duration of the journey to Surrey.

At the end of which you would have to be bodily extracted from the sidecar. Your legs would be tingling with pins and needles, the result being that you walked around, for at least an hour, like some over-exaggerated impersonation of Charlie Chaplan, much to the delight of the other members of the family.

Your one thought during the entire visit with Mick would be that you would not be the family cushion in the sidecar for the return journey.

Next came my sister Camilla, called Meal for short. Meal was six months older than I so we had much to share being the same age. Meal was a bit of a tearaway as a young girl, and didn't and still doesn't allow people to over rule her.

Last was my sister Ernestina. Tina was four years younger than me, and when we were children we felt, well I did, that she was spoilt. But being the youngest why shouldn't she be! It goes with the position in the family.

My school days were not the highlight of my life. I seemed to be mocked a lot for wearing glasses. I didn't consider myself a good scholar, but I have recently been given a school report that my mother found amongst her bits and pieces, which stated that I was first in the class. I didn't ever remember being first but it's there in black and white. I was about 10 and a half at the time - what a surprise.

I had a flair for sports and I loved being in the choir. Once a year the school would put on a light opera for the parents. I remember being in Haiawatha and Merry England.

My sister Meal and my friend Janice were also in the productions. I can well remember the excitement building as the first night came closer and closer - maybe I should have been an actress!

One fond memory I have was to do with my Nan. We lived at No. 23 in The Avenue and my Nan lived at 119. The Winter mornings are very cold in England - we would start our days by getting up and all hudding round the gas stove in the kitchen trying to warm ourselves and our clothes.

As I mentioned before, Doll would have our breakfast ready, of the usual porridge, and we would get that down us and then all troup to school with our play lunch of jam sandwiches in our hands.

By the time we arrived at Nan's house which was all of 10 minutes away, we would be frozen. She, bless her, would have waiting for us, a bowl of warm water to put our hands in and a penny each for the tuck shop at school.

She is gone now, but I wonder if she realised, I'm sure she does, how much we appreciated her kindness in those days at school -

hard and difficult days for the family, especially the children. My sister Meal, when things became too much for her at home, usually in the middle of one of the many family fights, would escape out of my brother's box room window, slide down the roof, which was over the porch at the front door, and run up the road to Nan's. Mum and Dad would soon stop quarreling and go and fetch her. It was a good ploy now I think about it to stop the fighting for a little while.

I met Dave, my husband, at one of the many dance halls in Romford. Meal and myself would go there on a Saturday night and on the off chance pick one of the halls that seemed more livelier than the others. We would pay our money and in we would go.

Dave had long sideburns and horn rimmed glasses, he looked a little like Hank Marvin from the Shadows. After nearly thirty years of marriage, I guess we were meant for each other, mind you there has been some rearranging on both sides.

After our marriage we moved to a little coastal town called Leigh-on-Sea. We had a rather large flat over the Chemist shop in the High Street. We were not there very long because within a few months I fell pregnant.

We decided to move to Brentwood as I felt that I would be more at ease closer to the family.

The baby was a boy and we called him Stephen. What joy he brought to us, and our lives really blossomed with this little one to cement our marriage.

After a couple of years of marriage we decided to look at the possibility of emigrating. We were living in a Council prefab at the time and we felt that we were becoming quite trapped and in a rut with our lives.

We didn't really see much future for ourselves and any other children that we may have. That was our feeling as a young couple.

We looked at going to either New Zealand or Australia, but there was a waiting list of two years before we could go and, like so many youngsters, we wanted to do it straight away.

So we went to South Africa House, and sure enough they were looking for Toolmakers, which was Daves' Trade, and they could indeed get us on to a boat within two months. So we decided, right, we'll do it.

You can imagine the reaction when we came home and told the in-laws and the out-laws that within 2 months we would be going to South Africa!

We said goodbye to our families at Charing Cross Station. Mum-in-law and Sister-in-law came with us on the train to Southampton. They saw us board the ship, up anchor and away.

I was 23, my husband 26 and little Steve was two. It was sad to say goodbye to everyone, but at the same time, we were excited at the thought of starting a new life in a land we had only read about and seen occasionally on news broadcasts on television.

Capetown was about four miles away when we woke up, on the morning of arrival, after having about two weeks of throbbing engines, the ship was suddenly quiet.

We all got up, dressed and went on deck. Once there, the Captain explained that the sight which was about to unfold before us all would be something we would remember for the rest of our lives - the sunrise over Table Mountain - and how right he was.

The morning was chilly, jet black and still. It was about four am. As we watched we began to see the twinkling of lights that seemed to sparkle like stars. Gradually more and more lights came on as the people in Capetown got ready for work.

As time ticked by we began to see the sun slowly rise behind Table Mountain and the scene was absolutely breathtaking. As there were no clouds or rain on that particular morning, the sunlight just shone so brightly that we could see quite clearly the outlines of the whole mountain.

The Captain said that on days when there is low cloud, Table Moutain appears a though it has a tablecloth on it, really a magnificent sight for anybody.

As we approached the harbour, we also began to hear the chattering of the Bantu Africans as they were preparing the ship for docking. It was a very exciting time for us and we were eager to be on shore and start the next stage of our lives in this new land.

Once on dry land again we waited for our luggage and the tool box to be uplifted from the bows of the ship. We were about to take the train from Capetown to Johannesburg that evening and Dave was anxious to have his tool box with him.

But horror upon horrors, as we watched his tool box being lifted by the crane from the ship, it swung over from the ship to the dock and came loose from the chain that was holding it and it dropped, smashing into the side of the wharf. The box split open, with all the tools scattering in every direction, then sunk to the bottom of the harbour. We could not believe it.

So here stood Dave, poor thing, with a wife and a little one, in a new country and the tools of his trade gone - what a start to our new life. There was nothing we could really do about it.

According to the insurance company we were not insured for the period of time the tools were lifted from the boat to the port.

The three of us boarded the train to Johannesburg that evening. The travel time would be two days and, thinking we could save some time in letting the families back in England know that we were okay, we decided to buy our postcards in Capetown and send them before we left.

We presumed, wrongly, I might add, that we should see many wild animals on our journey through the veldt so we picked cards showing zebras, lions and elephants roaming on the plains, and told the families that these were the animals we saw on our two day trip.

What a joke that was, all we saw was miles and miles of bright red earth and flat barren land. That taught us not to go counting chickens!

My main memories of Africa, that first few months, was the lovely climate. We couldn't believe that you could wake up every morning, day after day, to blue skies. Even as the years roll by, we still comment on it. It was a dry heat in Africa and my hair was bleached by the sun to a degree that it looked more auburn than dark brown. The two children we had in Africa, Stuart and Kathy, were white blonde.

Dave found work soon enough and so did I, our second son Stuart was born two years after our arrival.

I was eight and a half months pregnant with him when Steve, myself and this bump went to watch a soccer match my husband was playing in. It was only about a half hour drive from where we lived.

We had just moved into a new house and our household effects were still in the tea chests, we had only unpacked the essentials. We returned home to find that we had been burgled, they had uplifted the tea chests, stripped the beds and emptied the wardrobes.

Stuart was born two weeks later. After the burglary I only had the maternity dress I was wearing, so it was necessary for me to buy new maternity wear to see me through to Stuart's birth.

We could have done without this setback, once again we discovered that we were not insured at that time. We had given the change of address to the insurers but they maintain that the letter had not arrived at their office in time, so once again we were uninsured.

Well we picked ourselves up from that blow, more of life's experiences I suppose, a lesson well and truly learned - always read the small print on contracts!

Stuart was a joy to us all and Steve took on the role of big brother very well. The boys have always been close, and even though they are not so alike in their thinking, the basic love of family is always there. We had a good routine going with Stuart and Steve when Kathy came on the scene two years later.

Steve went to school near us, it was a small school which was run by Nuns who had come out from Brentwood in Essex to teach in South Africa. The school had no particular religion, children in Africa in those days started school at the age of six.

Steve said that his first day at school had been fine and that the teachers were "gnomes" which gaves us a good laugh. I was working, and we had a "nannie" to help with the children at home.

She told us one day that the school bus had pulled up outside our house to let Stephen off, and while one of the sisters was helping him down, our dog bounded up so excited at seeing Steve arrive, that he sent the nun flying - arms, legs, habit, the lot went rolling in the dust! She was completely covered in this red earth that is so much a part of Africa. The fact that she was knocked down and bowled over onto the ground, I must add, was such a delight to the other children on the bus. The sister picked herself up, brushed herself down and boarded the bus smiling and was on her way.

I must admit that I was nervous living in Africa with three children. It was compulsory that all doors and windows were fitted with burglar proofing. We didn't fit it, it was already there as a part of the home.

I did ask our nannie that if there was an uprising in Africa, would she harm us and the children.
"Oh no madam," She said, "You look after me, feed me and take

care of me; oh no, I wouldn't kill you."
She then told us that she would have no qualms whatsoever in going next door and killing the madam there and her family.

So it seemed to be a no-win situation, because while she was busy killing the people next door, the "nannie" from next door would be busy sorting us out - a worrying thought!

Before I leave my recollections of this great continent, though we had only seen a speck of it in comparison to its vastness, I will touch on the healing aspects of the Bantu African.

There was ample evidence that the tribes possessed some special healing powers - many times, while we were there, we heard how little sick white babies, whose parents had given up all hope of their recovery and were at the limits of desperation, would be given to their African maid.

The maid would take the child into the veldt or bush area and the tribe would perform some kind of ritual over the child, then the maid would return the little one to the parents.

No money ever changed hands. A good many of these little ones would begin to recover at a fast pace. I feel that they called upon all the universal power, the God power, to assist them and that the medicine man had this special something that could channel this power through him to the children.

I don't know. What I do know, however, is that on ninety percent of the children it worked.

I have, since becoming aware of the spiritual worlds myself, researched the different religions and beliefs of many nations and their people. Bantu Tribes, as far as their spiritual lives are concerned, tell of a Creator that forms men in the fields. How, nobody knows, but nevertheless, they have one. Their ancestral spirits were more important and far more active than those of the white man.

The African Ancestor would, in most cases, take the form of a small snake and thus remind the people of their presence.

Trees, flowers, the sky, the sea, and indeed all life contained these spirits, so the land was looked upon as sacred.

Medicines were made from the plants and juices squeezed from different herbs, then mixed with stream or sea water, and applied to the wound. It was sometimes given to hold in the mouth, then spat out as the healing was in the ritual, not so much the medicines or ointments.

Rituals took the form of a group of Africans surrounding the patient, chanting the names of the ancestors. They would work themselves into a fenzy and the Witch Doctor would be the channel for this all prevailing power. The patient would then be approached by the Witch Doctor and these herbs anointed or taken by mouth. The ritual would take hours, but as I mentioned before, the healings were successful with a large majority of the people, white or African.

Speaking more on spiritual matters, when I was working for a large firm in Johannesburg, the girls in the office and myself decided that we would go and see a fortune teller.

I was heavily pregnant with Kathrine at the time. We duly went in our lunch hour, paid our fifty cents and had a reading. I was told many things about coming into money and this and that which I took with a grain of salt.

The thing that did shake me though was that the man giving these readings asked me to stay behind because he said it was very important that he talked to me about the light and the spiritual realms. I didn't stay behind, I took off and went back to work with the other girls.

A few weeks later, while I was on the train to Johannesburg, I saw this man again. He was in the same crowded carriage as I was and I prayed he wouldn't see me but he did, I should have known that he would.

He couldn't have missed seeing my white face and the nervous expression on it. He would have been drawn to it like a moth to a flame.

The fortune teller approached me and once again spoke about the light and these other realms. He frightened the life out of me - I said I was on my way to work and couldn't spare the time.

He gave me his new address in Johannesburg from where he was doing the readings and I thanked him but had no intention of going to see him. As I left the train I tossed the address in the first bin I came across.

I will mention here about the light and these other worlds, briefly though, as I shall be going into them more thoroughly later in the book.

He would have told me that I was clairvoyant, which meant that I could, at times, see those spirits and teachers in the inner world, the place where we go at death. And that I was clairaudient, in other words I could hear voices, music and any sound that comes from this inner world. Clairsentient is being able to just know that a spirit or teacher is near me.

These are all part of the spiritual body and can function NOW! - while we are alive, there is no need to wait till death.

The light that this man was talking about is, as far as I am concerned, the inner white light that many see when they are about to fall asleep. This is the light of soul which shines into the other realms, much like the headlights of a car.

The decision was made to move on from Africa. Dave had written after a job in Australia, Sydney to be precise. So, once again we boarded the train, this time from Johannesburg, back to Cape Town. This journey was quite interesting and it had a very good start. We had a compartment that had three bunks each side, very close together. We bedded the children down, Steve on the top bunk, Stuart in the middle and Kathy below. My husband and myself were opposite them in the other bunks.

The train took off with an almighty shunt, to such an extent that Stuart flew off the middle bunk. Kathrine, watching all this, decided to throw her bottle of milk out the window. Dave, trying to catch the bottle, banged his head on the roof of the carriage. It wasn't funny at the time but whenever I remember it and see it in my mind's eye I think it's hilarious.

So off we went on this journey, no bottle for Kathrine who was all of eighteen months and with a nice collection of bumps and bruises between us.

Before we sailed from Cape Town we had a whole day to fill in. We decided to take the cable car to the top of Table Mountain, as we may never have the opportunity again.

The view from the top was once again breathtaking. The city seemed nestled at the foot of this majestic beast, the sun glistening on the sea which stretched out to infinity, with the ship below at anchor, and once again a brilliant sunny day.

The journey to Australia was fine except for our family managing to block all the outlets of the toilets on our particular deck by Stuart deciding, for no good reason, and never having done it before, to throw an apple down the toilet.

All the children on board seemed to be well behaved except mine. We cringed apologetically and asked forgiveness of the sailor who had to mop out and clear the toilet for us.

Steve slipped over on board early one morning, hitting his head on the deck, and was severely concussed. He was kept in the ship's hospital for some time and there was talk of putting him ashore at Fremantle, Western Australia and transferring him to a hospital. Fortunately he recovered well, but as soon as we landed in Sydney we had him thoroughly checked out.

We settled for a while in Sydney, buying a unit there. Dave found his job very slow and felt it was time to look again. This time we all moved to Newcastle about 150 kilometers north of Sydney and we soon found a house to rent in Belmont, by Lake McQuarrie a suburb of Newcastle.

Our neighbours were a young couple with a little girl of about five and a boy aged two; the children's Grandfather, Henty, who had a club foot, also lived with them.

We were welcomed by them and Henty took over the role of Grandfather to our three children. He was such a fine man, he would often cut the boys' hair and babysit for us.

He had a little section in his garden where he would grow vegetables which he tended with loving care - he would keep us in fresh vegetables for nearly the whole year round.

He was marvelous with wood carving and he made Kathy a lovely hobby-horse for one of her birthdays.

Henty told us that when he was very small, a few weeks old, his mother, who he loved dearly, was looking after the cattle while his father, a drover, was away.

One day the cows got themselves stuck in the creek so his mother had to go and shoo them out. She was holding Henty in a shawl in her arms at the time. One of the cows became agitated and pushed her, making her slip over. The baby fell out of her arms as she hit the ground and the cow's horn pierced his little foot, breaking it.

In those days, Henty said, doctors were many miles away and it would take many hours to visit them. His mother had done her best and hoped that all would be well.

He never saw a specialist in those early days, but when he was in his twenties, he decided to go and find out if he could sort this foot out. The surgeon said that the best thing they could do was to amputate the foot, so he decided that he would rather keep his foot as it wasn't too painful for him.

He wore a special built-up boot on the injured foot, which cost him a fortune to have made. This gave him his correct height. Henty wore this kind of boot for the rest of his life. He was a great friend of the family and we continued to write to each other until his death a few years ago.

Henty's club-foot had always bothered me, it seemed such a shame that this dear man should have to suffer so.

We wrote for many years as I have mentioned. One night I had a dream; I saw Henty and he looked about thirty, where in reality he was eighty. The most surprising thing I noticed was that he had two good feet, the clubbed foot wasn't there. Somehow I seemed to know that deformed bodies were perfect in this inner world.

I wrote to Henty about it and he wrote back saying, "If only it were true".
I couldn't convince him about it at the time, because it was all new to me. The real proof for me came later in my life.

After two and a half years we decided we would go home to England, so we packed our bags, put the house that we had bought up for sale and we were on our way.

We arrived in England in the middle of August 1971, after being away for seven years. The children's ages were, Stephen nine, Stuart six and Kathrine four.

Mother-in-law had re-married since we had been away, we only knew her new husband from the information we had gleaned over the years. We knew that he never had children of his own, let alone grandchildren. So we warned our children to be on their best behaviour while living in their Grandparents home.

Well, we didn't have to worry, what a lovely man he was, he used to bring them home toys nearly every day from his work. On weekends he would take them blackberrying or for long walks in the woods near their home.

I soon found Janice, my friend from school days, she and her husband had bought a lovely bungalow in Hornchurch. They now had another daughter and on the day we arrived they were busy painting the inside of their home. She looked fine and was very pleased to be nearer her Mum and Dad who were only a short bus ride away.

I found work in one of the big supermarkets as a cashier and I phoned Jan from the phone box outside the supermarket, as we didn't have a phone at home, to let her know that I would come over to see her the following week on my day off.

She told me that she had become ill while out shopping and in fact one of her friends had taken the two girls from her while she rested for a couple of hours. She said that she thought it was just one of those things and that she would be okay. So I told her to take care and that I would see her the following week.

That weekend we had a friend of Jan's husband call at our house to tell us Jan had died during the week.

As we didn't have a phone, it had taken the family quite some time to find us. It now seemed that my phone call to Jan was on the very morning of her death.

We were shocked to hear that her death was caused by a baby forming in the fallopian tube which was not investigated in time.

Jan was 31 years old when she died leaving a heartbroken husband and two young daughters aged seven and five.

My view on a God of love and mercy changed from that day onwards, some God I thought, who needs him if this was how he treated his children.

A few weeks later I had gone to bed and was still furious at this God we all seem to look up to. I was surprised to find that although my eyes were closed, I could see the room. The time, I knew, was about one thirty in the morning, and by rights the room should have been pitch black.

I could see the dressing table, the curtains, carpet, ceiling and anything I focused on. The room was still dark with no light coming in from outside and yet I seemed to be able to see! That was all there was to it, there was no way I could explain it, only that it happened.

While I watched and wondered about this phenomena, Jan seemed to come towards me - from where I couldn't say, it was as if she was walking through a country pathway straight into my bedroom. That is the only way I can explain it.

Strangely enough I was not frightened, in fact I was so pleased to see her I asked her how she was. She said for me not to worry about her, she was fine. She looked lovely and it was as if she brought her own aura of peace with her.

I recall that I didn't say anything, yet she seemed to answer my thoughts as they occured. This way of communicating with spirit was verified later on in life.

She seemed to fade then and I guess I must have fallen asleep. Little did I realise then that Jan would play a major role in my spiritual development in the years to come, giving proof of continued life not only for herself but for all.

Part Two

Contents

PART TWO
1. New Zealand

Our eldest son was now fifteen, we decided then to move to New Zealand. The spirit world opened wide at this time after the death of my father.

2. The Lifting of the Veil

Strange things begin to happen to me and I frantically look for an answer.

3. Church

My search for answers leads me to the Free Spiritual Church.

4. First out of body experience

While my physical body sleeps I move around in the spirit body.

5. The Spirit Teacher appears

The teacher manifests slowly and speaks to me.

6. A slightly confused Spirit

A young man needs a little coaching as he will not believe that he is dead.

7.   Jan begins to teach me

I am taken to a hall in the spirit world to be shown the help that the newly dead receive.

8.   My brother Mick is killed

Mick is killed instantly in a car crash. I am shown what happens from the spirit side when these accidents happen.

Once you catch the travel bug it becomes hard to stay in one place too long.

Our eldest son was about to leave school and there didn't seem much of a future going for the children in England, so we decided to move to New Zealand.

My family, Mum, Dad and the other members all had, over the years, one by one emigrated to New Zealand with their marriage partners and children.

Once again it was goodbye to Dave's side of the family, this time we left by plane.

The family duly arrived in New Zealand on the 20th August 1977. We had the usual mishap that even now happens - where the luggage goes on one plane and you and the family go on the other.

So, like so many others, we had to wait a day for our clothes etc, to arrive. We were welcomed at Auckland Airport by the family, Mum, Dad, sisters and many nieces and nephews I hadn't seen 'in the flesh' so to speak; I had only seen photographs of them. It was really wonderful to see them all.

My family had rented for us a dear little house out in Henderson. They had filled it with furniture, warmth and love.

The pantry was full of food and so was the fridge. My younger sister Tina had even lent us her car and there was really everything a family needed to start them off in a new country.

We were overwhelmed by their kindness. Each one of them had

put something into the house and it really did help us to feel at home right away.

We found our life in New Zealand to be, at first, much slower than we were used to in England, coming from a busy well populated town in Essex. The first thing we noticed was that streets and shopping areas were relaxed, easy going and nothing seemed to phase the New Zealanders. The motorists were patient with each other, and all in all an "It'll be alright" attitude prevailed. Refreshing, once we got used to it.

Now, after being here for thirteen years we find that life is busy and bustling. How we would fare back in England now, I have no idea. We would probably find it too hectic.

Our first year in New Zealand was mostly spent settling the children in school and finding employment for ourselves.

Nothing happened as far as spiritual experiences were concerned until my father became ill in the August of 1978.

Dad had become very listless and was eating very little so he took himself off to the doctor. The first verdict was that he had jaundice, then he was told that the symptoms were more in line with hepatitis. After many blood and other tests cancer was diagnosed.

Dad was taken into hospital and operated on for cancer of the bowel. He died six weeks later. It was a shock to us all.

It was just over a year from the August that we arrived in New Zealand to the October the following year when Dad died. I am thankful that we had a year together and I was able to get to know him again.

When I visited my Dad in hospital with the rest of the family, he used to say to us that he saw his mother and his brother and that when he saw them, it was reality to him. His mother and his brother had died many years ago, the latter in the war and the former, some ten years before Dad got sick.

He said to us that when we came to visit him it was as if we were in a haze or in a dream he was having. We were not as clear to him as when his mother and brother appeared.

Not being aware of the spirit, life after death and all the teachings in that line of thought, I found it quite worrying and scary.

He also mentioned that he and other patients would, of a night-time, walk around the hospital. But we knew that Dad couldn't even get out of bed on his own. All the family found Dad's behaviour very strange and worrying. Some put it down to the drugs he was on, but he wouldn't take them half the time and would rather bear the pain.

I, myself didn't think too deeply on it but I did wonder if there was an explanation for it all. And there was: Astral travel or spirit travel goes hand in hand with the near death experiences. These days this subject matter has been written about quite freely and investigated by many prominent doctors and psychiatrists.

A leading name in this field is Doctor Raymond A. Moody. Two well known books by this author are: "Life After Life" and "The light Beyond". Another excellent book is: "Beyond Endurance" by Glin Bennett.

When Dad died, I was relieved that he was out of the pain and suffering but also, that this dominating character was out of my life. I know that it sounds very unkind to say these things, but I'm sure that there are many of you out there who have family members that can cause quite a lot of friction within a household. Dad was such a person.

The funeral was over and we all went back to our various homes. Somehow, I felt that although Dad was dead he may still be able to rule from beyond. Doubt and fear started to consume me.

I felt that his character was far too strong, that even death would not release me from the hold he seemed to have on me.

So when I did start to see and hear the spirit world I became frightened, somehow I knew it had something to do with Dad; and I was right.

But looking back, I see he was trying to get help for himself and he had no intention of scaring me.

One night, roughly eighteen months to two years after Dad's death, I began to have some very strange and frightening experiences.

I was taught as a child to say my prayers at night, and even after Jan's death I continued the habit, that was really all it was - habit.

This particular night, what started to happen was that as I closed my eyes and began to drift off to sleep, I would start to hear whispering around me; voices, yet nothing clear.

While this was going on I felt as though I was going to swoon or faint. But something within me urged me to hold on and fight that feeling, which I did.

I seemed to have two bodies and each were pulling against the other, once I had woken myself up, i.e. wide awake, the feeling and the voices would stop.

Night after night this continued. I would force myself to wake up and go make myself a coffee and have a cigarette to calm myself down. Only then could I return to bed and be able to sleep.

I noticed that the time was twenty to two when these things would happen, the same time each night.

I became petrified of going to bed and would make up excuses for staying up late. I didn't tell any of the family, I didn't want to worry them so I kept it all to myself - rightly or wrongly.

I was becoming exhausted and, after six weeks of this, I decided, what the hell, if I was going to die I had better get it over and done with.

I decided that I would let myself faint the next time or do what ever it was that was required to rid myself on these sleepless nights.

I started in the usual way by saying my prayers and sure enough the swirling and voices began.

So I let it go, my head began to buzz and I began to see a mist around me which seemed to be coming from me. It was as if I had walked into a November fog, the thick kind that you would experience on a wintery evening in Britain.

But it was different, there was not the cold and damp you would usually associate with such a fog. It was still a mist which I could not see through.

I was part of it, from within and without, at the same time. The voices began and I found I could now understand them, I could make out the words that were being spoken.

The voices were male and female and were asking, "Can we use her now?" The same question was repeated, over and over.

Finally a woman's voice, quite calm and gentle in tone, said, "No, not yet." With that the whole place calmed down and I was, once again, myself.

Thank God that is over, I thought, and started to relax thinking I had come through the experience rather well, considering. Then the lady's voice spoke again. "Good night" she said, and hearing that I put my head under the blankets and went to sleep.

I worked at the time as a Supervisor of Accounts Payable in a large firm in Auckland and I had, in the office, three young girls under me. We used to talk about this and that, as you do in daily life.

I didn't tell anybody about what was going on at home, I kept it to myself. One day, one of the girls said that there was a new book out by a lady called Doris Stokes. She said that this particular lady was English and that she had come over to New Zealand the year before and had been on television and radio talk-backs. She had written a book called: "Voices In My Ear".

I said to the girls, "What does this woman do on the T.V. and radio?" and they replied, "She is a medium. She teaches, but she also gives demonstrations of clairvoyance."

They decided to buy the book, so I said I would have a copy too. We all got our books and off we went to our respective homes and had a read.

This lady spoke of another life, in addition to the one we live. She talked of the spirit world, the place where we go after death. She also said that when we die we do not change into some beautiful angel, full of wisdom and compassion, but we are exactly the same as we were before we died.

If we are a gentle person then we remain one. If we are a dominationg person, we remain so.

The physical body is dropped at death so she said. The spirit body survives in this other realm. Without the spirit body, the physical body does not function, which seemed logical to me because, at death something definately takes off and the physical body cannot move. So I found it all very interesting.

She also spoke of communication between this other realm and the physical world that we live in and that some people are able to do this.

She was one who could give clairvoyance. In other words, she could sense, hear and even maybe see those in this other realm of life. All very interesting I thought.

This lady also mentioned that sometimes those who pass or die have unfinished business on the earth and they do sometimes come back to find help for those who are living and for themselves.

Sometimes they themselves cannot communicate too clearly and it becomes a bit muddled. I thought to myself, this sounds a lot like what is going on in my house.

Doris wrote in her book of going to different churches, different places where she gave these teachings and this clairvoyance. The particular church that she did go to in England and was actually visiting here in New Zealand, was the Spiritualist Church. I thought, okay, then this is where I've got to go, to find an answer to what is happening to me.

I searched for one in Auckland and in the end I found one very close to where I lived in Te Atatu. It was called "Free Spiritual Church". Apparently there were twelve to fourteen churches in the Auckland area. So, my plan was, to go there the following Sunday evening.

I made sure I would arrive at the church in good time so that I could watch the other people going in. The date was 22nd February 1981.

I parked my car across the road from the school hall in which the service was to be held. A placard outside stated that the service would begin at 7 o'clock and that there would be clairvoyance and spiritual healing.

The members in my family were not pleased that I had made this decision and I was given a fairly cool send-off from home. I was nervous myself - but I had to find out just what was happening to me.

The people who entered the hall all seemed happy and chatty. They looked relaxed and eager to be in and seated, so at the last moment I decided to go in.

I got out of the car, locked it and walked across the road and in I went. Little did I know then that this was the start of an endless search for the truth about God, life, death and all that being on earth encompasses.

I was welcomed at the door by two of the church committee and then I seated myself in the hall right at the back. By the time 7 o'clock came around there would have been sixty people, by my estimation, waiting for the service to begin.

On the school stage facing us there was a table that had a blue cloth on it and over that cloth was a lace cover. On this there was a picture of Jesus. Both sides of the table bore a lamp with a blue light eminating from it. Beside the picture of Jesus was a model, about eight inches tall, of the 'Healing hands' and a beautiful bowl of flowers.

The service began with the pastor, or chairperson, welcoming everybody and saying a prayer for each one of us there plus the families we represented. Which I thought was a lovely thing to say and I felt a little more relaxed with the proceedings.

Then we had the Lord's Prayer and a hymn was sung. The hymns throughout the service were cheerful and I enjoyed singing them.

Next came the address, or lesson, I cannot recall the subject now. Then came a very interesting part of the service - Spiritual healing. This was something new to me at the time.

The pastor asked if there were any people among us that would like some spiritual healing - if they did then would they sit on one of the chairs that were arranged in a circle in front of the congregation.

Some people left their seats and came forward and sat in the chairs. The pastor then asked the resident healers to come forward and take their places, each one behind one of the chairs that was occupied.

A prayer was said and during this the pastor invited the healers and teachers of the spirit world to come close. The healing power would then be channelled or passed through the healer standing behind the chair to the one requiring healing.

Peace prevailed while this was going on and I noticed that the people giving the healing had their eyes closed. This made me a little uneasy, but all in all it was interesting to watch.

Once the healing part of the service was over the clairvoyant stood up. She began to give messages from those who had died, yet still lived, in this spirit world.

She picked someone out of the congregation and began to tell them about themselves, and that their mother, father or whoever had died, was there with the clairvoyant.

The spirit was giving the information of their death and saying things through the clairvoyant like there was a birthday or some anniversary coming up and that the spirit would be thinking of them on the day.

Most of the information was correct according to the person picked from the group.

This seemed strange to me, she went from one person to another and everyone seemed well pleased with what they received. When she finished, a prayer was said, the meeting closed and a cup of tea was served for all.

I felt quite at peace and I thought to myself, these people all look quite normal to me, none of them look weird and they are not worried about some spirit 'getting them'.

I finally plucked up enough courage to actually talk to one of the people there and tell her what was happening to me. She said that what I should do was imagine myself surrounded by a band of white light and ask whatever it was that was trying to communicate with me for a reason why and to ask what it wanted. So I thought I would do it.

By the time I got home that evening I felt quite uplifted from the experience and thought, well, I seem to be getting some answers here and I'll probably go to that church again. I will also put into practice that which I was told to do.

So that evening after getting everything ready for work the next day, I got into my bed and started saying my prayers. The old familiar things started to happen - the swirling and the whispers. I said, in my mind, not out loud (after all I had a husband lying beside me who would have thought I had really gone crackers!) "Could you please speak a little clearer, I cannot hear you".

At that, the noise of the whispering became so loud that I leaped out of bed. I was so frightened I suppose, I didn't know what to do with myself.

Dave wanted to know what my problem was, but of course I couldn't tell him, so I made some excuse about it being something else and off I went downstairs for the familiar cigarette and a coffee.

But the point was, there was some reaction to my asking.

The next Sunday I was ready. This time I didn't sit outside the church, I marched straight in because I wanted some more answers.

I started to go to these services regularly and listened to the wisdom that they were teaching. I also started to read a few books on the subject - but I was still having this problem at night.

In August of that year, 1981, I came back from Australia, after being on holiday there with my daughter, with a purpose in mind - to find out exactly what was going on. One of my sisters had seen my father since he had died and she was very frightened about it.

At the time of her experience I had joined a group that was teaching us how to become aware and to control the visions we were having and the power we were feeling. It was to this group that I brought the problem of my sister's experience.

We all used to discuss these things, one to another because it helped us to bring it down to a normal level, not something fantastic that was happening but something very normal and very down to earth.

I spoke about this experience and once again I was told that there was indeed someone around and that it was my father. Apparently he had some unfinished business to do on the earth and it was to do with me - my father, it seemed, was trying to tell me something.

These whisperings I was hearing and my sister seeing Dad were linked.

Our circle, or meeting, was run by a lady called Vicky. She had a brother who was a medium, so it was to this medium we all went to as a group. We had an evening where this medium told us, through the spirit help, that Dad had indeed been around and that we were all to say a prayer for him so that he would go to the realms of spirit where he belonged.

So this is what we did. We asked that Dad would go towards the light with our love and that all was forgiven, if there was forgiveness to be given, and that was that.

I returned home that evening and I went to bed, expecting, I might add, the whispers etc. to start.

They did not and have never returned since then. So that was another pointer towards some answers that this medium, with the help of the Guide, as they called him, had given me another valuable lesson in understanding the power of spirit.

I was also told that the swirling within me would continue, that it was nothing at all to do with Dad. It was to do with my own spiritual awareness, my own awakening into these realms of light and that this would continue. I was told not to worry about it and I was to just relax and let it go - to let it happen.

It didn't occur again for about a week and when it did I was ready. I relaxed, knowing that I was safe and that there was no way that I could be harmed because each and every one of us has a guide, or guardian angel, to look after us at all times.

The swirling feeling became very strong and I began to be aware of a loud buzzing in my head. I still didn't panic and then, suddenly, it all stopped and a calmness prevailed.

I found I was standing beside my bed, but I didn't remember getting out of it. I looked back at the bed and there, to my utmost surprise, was me, fast asleep.

I thought this very strange, because I was quite sure that I was wide awake when the swirling had begun, but there I was asleep.

Right, thought I, this is my chance to check all this out. So I decided to go and see my daughter who was asleep in the bedroom at the back of the house.

Once more I checked to make sure that I was still asleep - which I was - and moved towards the bedroom door, checking yet again to see that I hadn't got out of bed, then I went on my way, along the passageway towards Kathy's bedroom. As I went along, I passed the boys' bedroom, which was closed.

Now, I thought, if I am in this spirit body that I have been reading about and people have been talking about, I should be able, at this finer vibration, to go through any earthly object, including a closed door.

So, in for a penny, in for a pound, I walked forward and straight through the door and saw in the bedroom, both my boys asleep in their beds. I was so shocked that I actually did this, that I woke up in bed.

This was a real breakthrough for me. This showed that I could move and think very well without the use of a physical body, that I had at least two bodies, and who knows, I may have more.

I was now well equipped to answer some of the questions that others feel reluctant to think about let alone speak about - other people who were just beginning to be aware of this other world and were fearful of it, like I had been. I wasn't now. I was beginning to find a new strength within myself.

I was becoming calmer in my life, able to cope easier with everyday worries. These worries seemed to become watered down to a degree where I could handle them, whereas before, I used to become physically ill with worry over money - or the lack of it, and with material things that I was sure that the family and I needed.

Somehow, they didn't seem so urgent and by releasing the need for them they came on their own accord.

Such as a four-bedroom house to rent, with a landlord who was happy for us to have our dog, Tramp; and a job that payed good money which was just across the road from where I lived. Once I stopped worrying about the lack of them, all these wants just started to turn up.

I was so wrapped up with this new awareness of spirit that I had forgotten to worry. Strange it may seem, but my life was turning around and I was pleased.

I was getting a good night's sleep and everything seemed fine. So from Doris Stokes' book to the church and with the gentle teachers in the realms, I was well on my way.

11 January 1982

These inner teachers soon began to show themselves to me. The first one appeared in the middle of the night. I was begining to wake from a sleep when I heard a man's voice say to me, "Don't be frightened child, please don't be frightened".

As I became more aware of my surroundings, it was as if I had double vision. I looked across the bed to the wall opposite and there I saw a tall man in a light coloured beige robe. He was bending slightly forward as if to make sure I heard his words.

I replied to him, "No, welcome friend". He then became very clear, the double vision disappeared and I could see him quite clearly.

The robe he was wearing covered him from head to toe, the hood was up and as he was leaning forward, I was not able to see his face as the sides of the hood blanked his face out.

Now I noticed that the sleeves of the robe were folded at the elbow, or just below and he had on his left wrist a bangle of silver. It looked like links joined together but they were thicker than the ones we see today. His skin was tanned. He was so real to me, it even felt like the presence of a human person.

I could see quite clearly the wall and the wallpaper around him because there seemed to be a glow of light emanating from him.

He spoke again, "I will always be with you, you must never fear the astral or inner worlds because I shall place around you, a cloak of protection while you do your work".

By this time I started to worry that Dave would wake up and see this person and probably try to hit the intruder! - I was very green to this sort of thing happening. The teacher suddenly left, and all was darkness again.

I was so angry with myself for taking my attention from him because there had been the opportunity for me to ask all my questions about him and this other world.

Looking back and recording the experience now, I realise that had Dave woken up, he wouldn't have been able to see the visitor, because I was seeing with spirit eyes, or, clairvoyantly.

When we speak to spirit it is by thought as I have mentioned. His thoughts to me, sound like a voice and mine to him. I suppose the best way to expain it is, as a telepathic communication - you pick up the message and you relay one back in the same manner, with no words actually being spoken.

14th January 1982

I seemed to be viewing a scene from the ceiling, that is how I felt. I was looking down on a rather large room and in this room were different people, all gathered into groups. They were dressed in black and discussing the death of a young man.

Moving from one group to another was a young man who was not dressed in black. He had a pair on jeans on, a white shirt and a pullover, which was knitted in a fairisle pattern.

He had a beard and he looked to be around about twenty six. He was trying to talk with the groups but the people could not see or hear him.

I could see him, so I actually went down into the room. Thoughts are actions in spirit; in other words, I willed myself beside him.

He soon became aware that I was there and that I could hear him and speak to him. I asked him what he was doing. He said he was trying to tell the people that he was not dead but no-one was listening to him.

I then explained to this young man that he had died and that yes, the people on earth would not be able to hear him because they were in a different body than he was.

He had been in the physical body but now that he had died, he was in the spirit body. The people on earth would, therefore, be unable to see or hear him.

At first he thought this quite strange, but I said, "Look, hold my hand and we will go", and as we turned around, the wall of the room we were in disappeared and there was the most beautiful scenery in front of us - beautiful lush green grass, mountains in the distance, sunlight and flowers everywhere.

We floated out of the room and into this scene. He was so astounded he said, "Look, we are floating, isn't this a marvellous feeling?" To which I agreed. As we went further away from that grief-filled home, we came into an area where there were some of his loved ones who had died before him. They greeted him and I left him there. Then I woke up in my bed.

26th January 1982

Once again, I was taken to the spirit realms in the spirit body while I slept. This time I was met by my school friend, Jan. What a joy it was for me to see her.

"I am your teacher for tonight Vi", she said, "I am going to show you one of the jobs I do - we don't all sit around playing harps and wearing wings, as you can see."

Suddenly, we were players in a scene; we floated over the streets of London, down below the night was dark and filthy. The wind was strong and the rain was beating down steadily.

The time was late, I would guess about three in the morning. The few people venturing out on such a night were having difficulty staying on their feet. They were popping in and out of shop doorways to shield themselves awhile before moving on.

We began to slow down and zoom in on an old tramp I thought was asleep. We landed gently beside him.

"Look closely Vi", Jan said and I gave the tramp my full attention. As I watched, the tramp seemed to have an extra body, which sat up, stretched a bit and stood up, leaving the other body on the ground.

"This man has just died", Jan said, "Now see what reaction we will receive when we speak to him."

The tramp saw us and said, "Rough night girls, better get yourselves home, no time to be out in this." Jan said, "We thought we might go in there for awhile," indicating a hall not far from where we stood, "and warm ourselves up before we go home."
"Good idea", said the tramp, "I'll come with you."

Light and warmth seemed to emanate from the open doorway of the hall as we got near. We moved towards it but just as we were about to enter Jan held me back and we let the tramp go ahead.

Seconds later we entered. What a sight opened up before me, the hall had seats arranged much like a cinema and there was indeed a screen that was flickering with some sort of film on it. In each of the seats sat a tramp or bag lady, the down and outs of our world.

Jan began to speak.
"These people have all died alone on the street or in some back alley. Myself and others from the spirit world gently usher them into this or another similar place where they don't feel threatened.

The astral plane, or world, is the first place the average person arrives in after death. It is a replica of the earth, this is where we are now."

She continued, "These people in this hall, are in their astral or spirit bodies - they are all dead. You, Vi, are in your astral or spirit body at this moment, but you will be returning to earth after I have finished showing you these things.

The hall is a spirit hall, as I have said, and it is a replica of an earth hall." I said to Jan, "Well what happens now - That tramp we spoke to believes he is still alive, how are you going to convince him that he is dead?"

"Watch", she replied, and as I watched, my new friend the tramp, was looking at the screen with a puzzled expression on his face. It was the same scenes over and over again being shown to him.

He was looking at himself sitting on the ground eating a lump of bread and drinking a bottle of stout. When he had finished he had tucked himself under his dirty old blanket and fallen asleep.

Then he watched himself wake in the same manner as Jan and I had seen - he saw his two bodies, he even saw himself speak to me and Jan.

Suddenly a light began to glow around him, and before I could say a word, Jan went forward and led him out of the hall.

Once outside, he said to Jan, "I gather I have died."
"That's right", said Jan, "Look around you and see if you can recognise anyone."

The dark street of London was gone and in it's place was a beautiful garden with soft music and a gentle warm breeze.

Seated on the grass and standing in groups were many people who turned their faces in welcome to this man. He shouted with obvious delight, "That's my mother, and over there is my older brother."

The next moment I was back on earth awake in my bed. What a brilliant night! I couldn't wait for my next lesson.

27th November 1982

I was sitting watching the television with the family that evening when I suddenly became aware of a power around me which seemed so very strong that I silently asked for help from the teachers to control it.

It was late in the evening, the feeling finally subsided and all was well. The family went to bed quite late and at about 1:30am we were awoken by the telephone ringing.

I answered the phone, a young man was on the other end and he wanted to talk to my husband.

My son Steve was out that night with his friend at a night club and I had that awful fear that something had happened to him. My husband answered the phone and it turned out to be my nephew to say that my brother Mick had been killed instantly in a car smash in Wellington.

I went through a mixture of emotions, it was a relief that it wasn't Stephen and then quite shattering because it was my brother. Anybody who has had such a phone call knows how it feels. Unfortunatley you cannot explain it.

The feeling has to be experienced to know the deep shattering blow that hits you emotionally.

Tina, Doll and I flew down from Auckland to Wellington, it was only a short flight, under an hour, in fact. My mum, sister Meal and her husband flew over from Melbourne, Australia and we all arrived at my sister-in-law Viv's home the following day - Sunday.

Life after death was really being questioned now by everybody. I knew all would be well with Mick but I did need some proof, as we all do.

I can honestly say that I did not shed a tear for Mick, worrying where he was. During that time at my sister-in-law's we all talked about our lives together and the memories of family, recalling the laughter and hard times of our youth.

We were all tired physically and emotionally so I decided to go to sleep. Viv's home was full of the family and we were bedded where ever there was room. Mum, myself and Tina were in the lounge and we each had a sleeping bag.

I said to them all that I was tired and that I would now be going to sleep. They were still chattering and talking away about this and that when I snuggled down into my sleeping bag and pulled the flap across my face.

I could still hear very clearly the traffic outside, the conversation going on in the living room and the odd dog barking, out in the night.

As I pulled the flap of the sleeping bag across my face, I began to see through the third eye, the inner vision began to open (the spiritual eye or third eye is the window between this world and the inner worlds - it is located between the eyes above the bridge of the nose. With eyes closed you can condition yourself to look through this light into the realms.)

I was not asleep and in this vision a scene unfolded. The night my brother died was a very wet, dark, raining, miserable night in Wellington but the picture I was seeing was in brilliant sunshine.

My brother was killed going over a small bridge in Wainuiomata, a town in Wellington, and I was shown that as his car approached this bridge, there came from the other direction a young man driving his car.

Mick's car was a silver colour, which I had forgotten up until now, and I saw it clearly.

Just before the two cars were about to approach the bridge there came a mist from the side of the driver's seat where my brother was. The mist began to form the spirit body of my brother.

Mick's physical body was changing gear in the car for going over the bridge; His spirit body was being welcomed by my father. They both looked back at the scene and watched the two cars crash without any emotion whatsoever.

It was as if they were going from the living room to the kitchen and maybe there was a cartoon or something on the television which they paused to glance at then carried on past.

This was how they looked at the scene below them, noticing it yet not worrying about the outcome, then they moved away from the Earth.

The two cars collided, but my brother was well away from it. So, this was interesting to see. I hadn't realised that this was what happened.

I have seen so many things in these inner realms but when it comes to the death of someone we love, it is not easy to take things so lightly. We want the truth, we don't want these gifts from the realms to be given to us and not be tested. I said a prayer of thanks and sent my love to Mick.

A few months afterwards I picked up a book that explained exactly what had happened. This book was written by a father whose son had been killed in a car accident with a young girl in South Africa. He had written of his experiences and how he managed to find some comfort in these other realms.

For those of you who grieve the loss of your son or your daughter, the name of the book is, "On The Death Of My Son", written by Jasper Swain. I am sure that you will be able to get this book at any of the shops in your area. There are many authors who write this type of material about life after death, the spirit realms, the universal self, whatever.

So, I was thankful; once again I had been given the proof that life continues after death.

Part Three

Contents

PART THREE

1. Looking Back.

The evidence I was given during that year had me hungering for more.

2. More Spirit Visits.

A list of journeys I have had over the years.

3. The Inner Teachers/Eckankar.

The relationship between the teacher and student. The ancient science of Soul Travel.

4. Near Death Visions.

These need to be explained.

5. Kathy.

My daughter is killed in a car crash.

6. Today.

The work is still to do, and lessons to be learned.

1982, What a year. I seemed to have been through just about every lesson on the spirit side of life - to do with death and dying anyay.

First the teacher in the robe arrived, and with him I went into the inner worlds to be shown so much. I have often heard that when the pupil is ready the teacher will appear. I must have been ready.

There was a reason for all this of course. It was to prepare me for my brother's death and, later on in life, that of my daughter's.

January was the month. On the 11th, the teacher, on the 14th, the young man, and on the 26th, my friend Jan. So what had I learnt?

That we can see and go into the inner realms, at will, and that when we have died we are the same mentally, in other words our thoughts and feelings remain the same.

When we have become aware of the other world, we settle down to help others and also to learn as much as we can of the nature of life in those realms. We are not idle, that's for sure, as Jan has shown us.

The main lesson that came across was that we live on after death, but in another dimension. That we are loved by our God and that communication between the two worlds can and does exist. We all have a spirit or soul body and it is this body that motivates us now.

When we leave this world we shall be free to express ourselves within that body, with no aches or pains, trials or tribulations. What a great awakening awaits us.

The fear of death had been taken away from me and I certainly look at life with brighter eyes. I am pleased to be alive and I intend to enjoy every moment of it.

We may part from each other physically at death, but not spiritually. For spirit and love continues. The connection is always there between those we love who have gone before us and we who are left here on earth.

The next few years I continued to be taught on the inner realms. I was shown what happens just before death once again.

This time, I was looking at a car speeding along with four young men in it. They were laughing and singing, their music blaring out. It looked as though they were going home, or from one party to another.

As I watched, the four young men rolled out of the car, landing on the grass bank beside the road, the car continuing on it's path. The spirits of the boys simply tumbled out through the closed doors.

They landed in a heap at the side of the road. Then it seemed as if they were just waking up, because they began to stretch and yawn and talk to each other, wondering where they were. Around them stood family members and friends belonging to each of them.

Another time I was shown a young girl of about 23 years. She had just had a car crash, I could see her body in the car, broken and bleedng.

Yet she, as the spirit, was bending down picking up her shoes. She put them on and just walked away. She didn't have a scratch on her and she looked full of life. She had long blonde hair and a very slim body . She was wearing a white and blue printed dress which was made of a very soft silk and she looked rather lovely. She certainly didn't seem concerned about the body in the car.

Three years ago (1986), I, like many other people, endeavoured to give an hand to one of the welfare groups, while still working to earn a living.

On this occasion it was one of the Children Societies. It seems that many of the societies these days actually deal with the older generation, children grow.

The lady I was asked to go and see lived in a suburb of Auckland called Mount Roskill. She was due to return to hospital on the following Monday, she was very ill and weak.

I was asked if I would sit with her awhile and maybe give her aching limbs a massage. This call I received at work on a Thursday, I was to visit the lady the following day after work at about three thirty.

My directions for travel have never been good, so I looked up the local map and planned my route for the following day.

That night I found myself in the spirit realms, once again I became part of a scene. I was in a room which had three sides, in front of me was a panoramic view of meadows and snow capped mountains. It was a beautiful sunlit day.

To my left there was a bed on which a lady was lying, beside the bed was a large comfortable arm chair. I was standing by this with one arm resting on the back, the room was obviously a bedroom. To my right stood three men which I felt sure were doctors or medical consultants.

They were not dressed in hospital gowns but in smart suits and they seemed to be discussing the lady's case.

I had no idea what was behind me, I had no reason to look, all the action was within my viewing space. The lady hopped out of bed and sat down on the chair that I was standing by.

I said to her, "Considering you live in a built-up area, this view you have is unbelievable." I knew for a fact that Mount Roskill did not have such a view in reality. The lady just smiled.

The three men stopped talking, turned towards us and addressing us both, one said, "We feel that you", he was looking at me, "should take the patient out for a pleasant walk in the sunshine, we feel she will then be fine."

The lady stood up from the chair, with no effort, I might add, and I led her across the room and out into the sunshine.

The next moment I was back in my bed at home on earth. The following day, about mid-morning, I recieved a phone call from the society to tell me that this particular lady had died very peacefully in the early morning.

At this time I feel it is right to talk about the helpers and teachers of the spirit world, of the heavenly world. Each one of us has with us a teacher, a guide, a helper.

The Roman Catholics are told that they are born with an angel to guide them through their lives. We all do have such an angel, or teacher beside us. They help when grief comes upon us and we are left here on earth with a heavy heart through sorrow.

There is always a band of these helpers that gather at the time of a bereavement and assist in the home. You will find, as some have already realised, that when you lose somebody you love there is a calmness that prevails, a peacefulness - so calm at times that you cannot believe it.

For about a week it is as if you have been slightly sedated. Not through drugs but by a healing power within the home. This is the presence of the comforter which is mentioned in the Bible.

Remember that we are never alone, there is always the love of the God force, of the spirit realms, of these angels, to carry us when our load is very heavy.

As I record my experiences and the teachings I have gained, much of it will seem very familiar to you because you, too, have been to these places and have seen much the same as I have seen.

Hopefully, it will give you the conviction that you, too, were helped at a certain time in your life, and taken to a peaceful place in the heavens so that you might carry on your daily life with a calmer and more positive attitude.

ECKANKAR is a movement that teaches Soul Travel, and becoming aware of the Light and Sound of God. I had been having out of body travel for some time, as well as seeing the white light and hearing the sound, or music, of the inner worlds.

I had joined ECKANKAR in the November of 1984, after reading a book on the subject written by Paul Twitchell, founder of ECKANKAR.

The book told of similar experiences to mine. The present day leader, Harold Klemp, was visiting New Zealand at the time and was to give a public talk on these topics at one of the main hotels in Auckland - so I went along.

There came onto the stage a very slim man who appeared to be in his mid thirties. He told us that the job of the Living Eck Master was to bring those souls who were ready, back to God by way of the Light and Sound.

He also said that within the Movement we are shown that we can leave the physical body at will, by looking into the light and chanting the names of God.

The main point that came across from him was that he not only taught on the physical realm, he also worked with us on the inner realms. I found this, to tell the truth, a bit too fantastic to even think about.

Therefore, I was duly surprised when on the morning of Kathy's death, on the inner realms I saw the face of this man come towards me just as I awoke.

So far as I am concerned this is a fact, and I am still with ECKANKAR to this day. Once again, one has to experience to know.

Note: The terms ECK and ECKANKAR are trademarks of ECKANKAR, P.O. Box 27300, Minneapolis, MN 55427 and are used herein with its permission.

In September 1984 I had a dream. I was in my living room and there was a knock on the front door. I got up, opened the door and there in front of me was a policeman and policewoman. They said to me, "Mrs Tasker, one of your children has been killed." I asked whether it was Kathy and then I woke up.

I didn't think too much about it because I knew Kathy didn't drive a car. However, both the boys did.

I thought to myself, well it could be me worrying over the fact that Kathy was coming to the age of being able to get her licence and would be wanting us to help teach her to drive. In fact, she was having lessons with her dad every now and then.I thought no more about it.

In the January of 1985 Kathy decided to go on holiday to Australia to visit her Aunty Meal. She had three weeks away. She returned the first week in February and was full of all the exciting things she had done.

She was seventeen and a half at the time. A couple of days before she came home I had another dream. Once again there was a knock at the door. Once again I went to open it but I felt that I shouldn't open it. I tried with all my might to push the door closed again but there was a power so strong behind that door that I found it very difficult and I woke up very disturbed.

A week later when Kathy was home, she was in the garden and she said to me, "Mum, is Dad home?" I said, "No love, he's at work." She said, "But I see Dad at the window upstairs in the hallway and he is waving at me."
"Well", I said, "he can't be love, because he is definately at work.

Come on, let's go and have a look." We both went indoors, upstairs to the landing. There was nobody there. So we left it at that.

My father-in-law and my husband look very much alike and I like to think that it was her grandad, who had died before I was even married, and had come to show himself to her and prepare her for what was about to happen.

Kathy worked for one of the large supermarkets in Henderson after school, as so many other youngsters do, to earn extra pocket money. That was until she obtained her permanent job as a Trainee Veterinary Nurse.

Her friends from school and the supermarket arranged for a trip to go "White-Water Rafting" and asked Kathy to go with them. The convoy left early on Sunday morning, Kathy included, on the 10th February 1985; they left on a lovely clear summer's day.

Sunday Morning 10th February

I found myself in the dream state. I was in a lovely valley, the grass and hills around me were more beautiful than I had ever seen. I was talking to many friends and family I had known on earth, who were now dead as far as those left on earth were concerned.

I did not find this difficult to accept because I knew by all my experiences in the spirit realms that we all go to the heavenly home in the end.

I was chatting away, I can't remember what we were all talking about, only that we were all very happy to be together. After a while I said goodbye to them and it was as if I was floating away from that scene. They were all smiling and waving goodbye as I drew away from them.

I must mention that there was beautiful music that I could hear very faintly all the time. The next moment I was placed very gently on an open deserted road or path, gold in colour, though not bold, it was more a soft pastel tone.

There before me stood my daughter Kathrine, looking up at me. She, as I looked at her, was about 4 and a half years old. I bent down and picked her up and cuddled her to me as mums do.

She put her little arms around my neck, her little legs around my waist and we just held each other like a mother and child, at that special time in life when the little ones feel so safe in your arms and you feel fiercely protective of them.

As I held her I began to be aware of the music. I could hear that there were no instruments at all, just beautiful voices singing. At first it seemed at a distance but as I stood there, the choir became louder and louder until it filled Kath and I with its magic.

The song the choir was singing was one my mum used to sing when I was young . . . "Love is the Sweetest Thing". I began to sing the words. Then, as I held Kath and the choir became part of us I woke up. The last person I saw as I woke was the face of Harold Klemp (The Living Eckankar Master).

When I woke I thanked the Master and the heavens for such a lovely visit to the realms. All I felt was unconditional love and peace that truly did pass all understanding.

I got out of bed and got myself ready. I was actually in the bath when the phone rang. I could hear Dave talking and the next minute he came running up the stairs. He said to me that it had been Thames Hospital on the phone and they informed us that there had been a car accident. Four young girls had been in the car - one of the girls had been killed instantly and Kathy was critical.

I flew out of the bath and quickly got dressed and within no time we were on our way to the hospital, which would be a drive of about two hours..

During the drive down we were talking about Kathy and wondering how she would be when we got there and all the other things that you talk about in a crisis like that. In a quiet moment I began to feel a very gentle sensation around my head on the left side.

I also began to hear the music of one of the pop groups that Kathy really loved. So I said to Kathy, with my thoughts, "Now darling, are you dead?" The thoughts came back to say, "No Mum, I'm fine, but I can see Uncle Mick and I can see Grandad."

Then the music ended and she was gone. I felt, deep, deep, down inside as if a cold iron hand had grabbed my heart and severed it. I wept silently within, as I knew at that stage, that she had left us.

When we arrived at the hospital, there were many young people there. A few of them were hurt, but I will never forget seeing their little white faces. This is mainly why I am writing this book - to give some comfort to the youngsters who lose friends, as well as the parents of the children who have died.

We arrived and were told that our Kathrine had passed, that she had been resuscitated once, but had then slipped away.

We were devastated. There's no doubt about that and we came home to our eldest boy in a daze. Our younger boy had gone away for two weeks on a teaching assignment. It was five hours before he could get home and we could all be together.

I don't have to describe what it is like to lose somebody so close or the sadness that fills the home. But looking back, I feel there was comfort given us, we were given a lot of strength at the time when we needed it.

I would like to talk further about the viewing of your life as you pass. I have mentioned it previously in the book. I like to feel that when I saw Kathrine at four and a half years of age that morning, spirit-wise, I felt that I was pulled toward her, and was able to pick her up at that age and help her across the border to the spirit realms.

We are connected in love within the spirit body and we are drawn to those we love, all of us. So many of you may very well have been with your loved ones at the time of their passing, at the time of their troubles, even though you may not realise it.

Both my boys have had ample proof of Kathy's continuing life in those realms, but it is entirely up to them how they feel about it. It is not my job, or anybody elses, to try and tell you how to grieve and tell you what is correct with communication from spirit and what is not.

But if people talk to you about seeing their loved ones, being with their loved ones, do not ridicule them because there is definately a push on the other side of life to bring that comforter close to those who grieve.

EARTH TO HEAVEN AND BACK

I'll lend you for a little time, a child of mine
He said, for you to love the while she lives,
And mourn for when she's dead.

It may be six or seven years, or twenty two or
three, but will you, till I call her back, take
care of her for me?

She'll bring her charms to gladden you and
should her stay be brief, you'll have her lovely
memories as solace for your grief.

I cannot promise she will stay, since all from
earth return, but there are lessons taught down there,
I want this child to learn.

I've looked this wide world over in my search
for teachers true, and from the throngs that
crowd lifes lanes, I have selected you.

Now, will you give her all your love, nor think
the labour vain?
Nor hate me when I come to call to take her
back again.

I fancied that I heard them say, 'Dear Lord
Thy Will Be Done'

For all the joy this child shall bring, the
risk of grief we'll run.

We'll shelter her with tenderness,
We'll love her while we may,
And for the happiness we've known, forever
grateful stay.

But, should the angels call for her, much sooner
than we've planned,

We'll brave the bitter grief that comes and try
to understand.

I have no idea who wrote this beautiful poem, whoever you are I would like to thank you on behalf of myself and the many bereaved parents who have found comfort in these words.

I myself have never had a near death vision, because I have never been in a stressful condition where my life was threatened at any time. I have read about them, however. I have also been told about them, from people I can trust, and I can definately say that they do occur.

What I have been shown, is what happens when a person passes or dies. The only difference between having a near death experience and actually dying is that when we die we do not return to the body, a body, most times, full of pain. We stay put in that realm of light.

And so it was with Kathy. Obviously she was worked on by the people in the ambulance, and at the hospital. The Doctor resuscitated her once, yet on my way to the hospital, I was quietly talking to her and she gave me her explanations of what was happening to her.

A book that I think you will find very interesting is by a psychiatrist, George G. Ritchie. The book is described as such - "A psychiatrist describes his own revealing experiences on the other side of life."

This is the story of a young man who was pronounced dead and how he was shown, by a being of light, what the other side of life was all about. He was also given a review of his own life. He was only a young man of twenty at the time and he was in training at an army base. He became a psychiatrist many years later.

The book is well worth reading.

And oh - the dream I dreamed that night
Was bathed in a great golden light -
I walked in this great light - and found
I trod strange, yet familiar, ground
For trees and flowers I once knew
Held colours of a brighter hue
And perfume - loving and so kind
That as I breathed caressed my mind -
I stood a while, then, everywhere
The sweetest music filled the air
It flowed into my aching heart
Leaving peace in every part
Then seemed to call me o'er a plain
Where a soft and gentle healing rain
Mingled with my tears - unshed
Until this music filled my head -
The golden light in brilliance grew
And in that wonderous light - was you

My only hope is that, with this book, some comfort has been given to those that grieve, and also a few answers for those of you who are searching for some understanding of the experiences you have been having.

Love and light to you all.

Vi Tasker
vtspiritenvoy@yahoo.com

REFERENCES

ECKANKAR
P.O. Box 27 300
Minneapolis
Minnesota 55427
America

Voices In My Ear
Futura Publications Ltd
Greater London House
Hamstead Road
London NW7QX

On the Death of My Son, by Jasper Swain
Publishers.
Turnstone Press Ltd
Wellingborough
Northamptonshire
England

Return From Tomorrow, by George G. Ritchie,
Chosen Books
The Zondervan Corp
Grand Rapids
Michigan 49506
America

Dr R M Moody
The Light Beyond etc.
Bantam Books
Your Area

Life After Death, by Neville Randall,
Transworld Publishers
Century House
61 - 63 Uxbridge Road
Ealing
London U.K.

www.ingramcontent.com/pod-product-compliance
Lightning Source LLC
Chambersburg PA
CBHW061502040426
42450CB00008B/1454